A M A Z I N G   A N I M A L S

NARWHALS

BY ASHLEY GISH

CREATIVE EDUCATION • CREATIVE PAPERBACKS

Published by Creative Education
and Creative Paperbacks
P.O. Box 227, Mankato, Minnesota 56002
Creative Education and Creative Paperbacks
are imprints of The Creative Company
www.thecreativecompany.us

Design by The Design Lab
Production by Blue Design
Art direction by Graham Morgan

Images by Getty Images/by wildestanimal, 6; Shutterstock/Catmando, 13, Dotted Yeti, cover, 1,18, 21, Saifullahphtographer, 5; Wikimedia Commons/A. Thorburn, 23, Cephas, 11, Dr. Kristin Laidre, Polar Science Center, UW NOAA/OAR/OER, 2, 7, Gazprom neft, 14, Gunnar Creutz, 16, Paul Gierszewski, 20, пресс–служба ПАО "Газпром нефть",9 , 17, Проектный офис Нарвал, 10

Cataloging-in-Publication data is available from the Library of Congress.
Library Binding ISBN: 9798895810569
Paperback ISBN: 9798896800095
eBook ISBN: 9798895811825
LCCN: 2025010733

Printed in China

Table of Contents

Narwhals (NAR-walls)

live in the icy waters of the Arctic Ocean. They are a kind of whale. Many people know them as "the unicorns of the sea." But the narwhal's "horn" is really a tooth called a tusk.

The tusk can be up to 10 feet (3 meters) long. Some narwhals have two tusks. This is very rare.

Usually, only male narwhals have tusks. Some experts believe narwhals can feel how cold or salty the water is with their tusk. Others think the tusk helps males impress females.

Adult narwhals have black and white spots on their back. Their belly is white. Baby narwhals are blue-gray. Old narwhals can be nearly all white.

Narwhals are not very big whales. They weigh up to 4,200 pounds (1,905 kilograms). They can grow to be 17 feet (5.2 m) from nose to tail. This is about half the size of an orca.

Narwhals swim to the water's surface to breathe. They breathe through a blowhole on top of their head.

The range where narwhals are found is small.

Narwhals live in a harsh **habitat**. The Arctic is dark and covered with ice for half the year. Many animals would die in the Arctic. But narwhals have thick **blubber**. It keeps them warm in the freezing-cold water.

habitat place where plants or animals live

blubber a thick layer of fat under the skin

If a person ate as much food as a narwhal, it would be like eating 200 apples in one day!

Narwhals eat about 66 pounds (30 kg) of food per day. Narwhals do not have teeth—their tusk is their only tooth. They swallow food whole. Their prey includes fish, shrimp, and squid.

prey animals that are eaten by other animals

Some other toothed whales are orcas, beluga whales, and sperm whales.

Narwhals live in groups called pods. There may be 15 to 20 narwhals in each pod. Living in pods helps them stay safe. Predators, like polar bears and killer whales, hunt narwhals.

predator an animal that hunts other animals for food

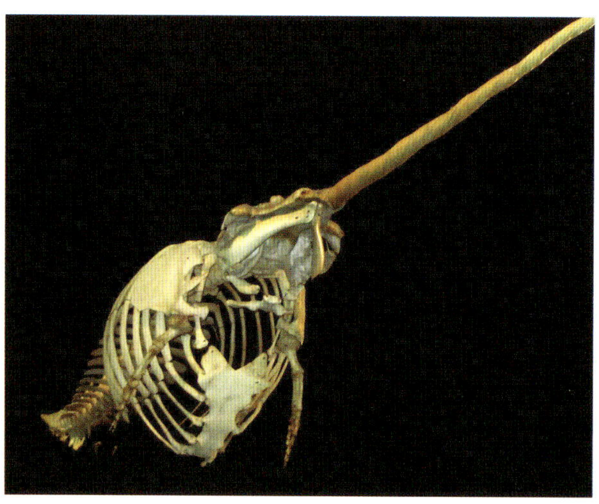

Narwhals find mates at the end of winter. Mothers give birth after 14 to 16 months. They have one **calf** every three years. Calves can swim shortly after they are born. Narwhals live for 25 to 50 years.

calf a baby narwhal

A narwhal may click up to 1,000 times per minute.

Narwhals have the best echolocation of any animal in the world. They make clicking sounds that bounce off things in the water. The echoes travel back to the narwhal. The narwhal uses the echoes to make a picture in its mind.

echolocation using sound to find things in the water or air

Narwhals need deep, cold water to live in. They can dive more than a mile (1,800 kilometers) underwater. They can hold their breath for up to 25 minutes! The only place to see narwhals is in the wild.

People hunted narwhals hundreds of years ago. The hunters sold narwhal tusks, claiming they were unicorns' horns.

A Narwhal Tale

An **Inuit** woman hunted a white whale. A boy wanted to save the whale. He pushed the woman into the sea. Her long hair twisted like a rope. She turned into a narwhal and joined the other whales.

Inuit the native people of the Arctic region

Read More

Jaycox, Jaclyn. *Narwhals Are Awesome*. Oxford: Raintree, 2020.

Markle, Sandra. *The Great Narwhal Rescue: Saving the Arctic Ocean's Narwhals*. Minneapolis, MN: Millbrook Press, 2025.

Orr, Tamra B. *Amazing Creatures of the Arctic Ocean*. Mount Joy, PA: Curious Fox Books, 2024.

Websites

Narwhal Facts and Pictures
https://kids.nationalgeographic.com/animals/mammals/facts/narwhal
Learn more about the amazing narwhal.

Narwhal
https://kids.britannica.com/students/article/narwhal/631207
Read more about what narwhals look like and how they live.

Index